A Mano / By Hand

Nicole Cecilia Delgado

Translated by Carina del Valle Schorske

There is no such thing as art and life—there's only life.

Ulises Carrión

Poetry is not a project.

Dorothea Lasky

To the memory of Esteban Valdés (1947–2020)

Eight years have gone by since I came back to live in Puerto Rico, the same number of years that I lived outside the country. It's hard to imagine a future from the present context, shut up in my rental apartment in Santurce during the global coronavirus quarantine. I dream of buying a big house where I can set up my workshop, La Impresora. Someday I won't owe rent to anybody. I want to live near the beach, establish a seasonal residency for writers and collaborators, and begin to create a network with nodes on other Caribbean islands. I want to grow vegetables, install solar panels, and build a cistern to store rainwater—all of this is part of the project. And of course, I want to continue making books of poetry.

I agree with Dorothea Lasky that poetry is not merely a project.[1] Rather, life itself, insofar as it permits the creation of poetry, is really the primary project. And the sustainability of life as a poet is without a doubt a difficult mathematical problem, a project of survival—even more so recently, as we bear witness to the collapse of institutions that used to be dedicated to education and art. The repercussions of these budget cuts have been severe for the sustainability of all kinds of cultural production.

This is what my daily quest is about. I'm calling up the stereotypical specter meant to scare young poets: *you're going to die of hunger.* But the challenge goes beyond not dying of hunger. The challenge—the project—is to live with dignity, to achieve real quality of life, to create community in the process and find joy doing so. The project is to live with/in poetry: poetry is the project's basic unity.

3

I

Ricardo León Peña Villa was a Colombian outsider poet
who lived in a house on the Lower East Side of Manhattan
in the nineties and early aughts. The building, tucked
between 2nd and 3rd streets on Avenue C, was known
as the Umbrella House. Ricardo was, I think, one of the
poorest people I've ever known. Also one of the most
generous. His apartment, #3D, was the refuge and meeting place for a vast menagerie of Latin American artists
who arrived in New York with or without papers. I
traveled into the city on weekends from Albany, where I was
studying for a Master's degree in Latin American Studies.
The university did not strike me as a productive site of
action. But in Ricardo's house there was a real network of
cultural exchange, beyond hierarchy and capitalist logic.
As in the popular story *Stone Soup*[2] with cooperation and
a little ingenuity there was always food for everyone—also
drinks, music, poetry, art, and love. Between Nuyorican
Manhattan and Colombian Queens, this impossible logic
supported the creation of many intergenerational DIY
projects: poetry marathons, individual and collective publications (like the magazine *Casa Tomada*), and a Spanish
language poetry festival that we celebrated for several
years running. Ricardo also threw some of the biggest and
most beautiful parties in the whole area. His project, without a doubt, was to live well in New York—while speaking
Spanish and writing poetry.

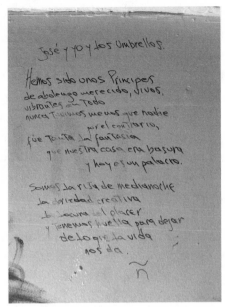

Improvised text by Peña Villa on one of the walls
of Umbrella House, circa 2008.

The project was going well, and the poetry was going well—thanks for asking. But capitalism played a trick on Ricardo. He died prematurely in March 2011, in large part because he couldn't pay the high price of medical care in the city.[3] I like to think of him as my first chosen teacher. Thanks to him I traveled to Colombia to publish my first book of poetry with a small, almost invisible press in Medellín that his friends had started. I was only twenty-three; I was not especially ready. But in the days of preparation for this trip, sitting in the living room of his apartment, Ricardo León urged me to write "poet" as my "occupation" on the customs form.

Soon after that trip, I learned to make books by hand thanks to Tanya Torres, a Puerto Rican artist and poet who had lived in el Barrio since she was a teenager. Tanya had training in printmaking, but during a battle with cancer she had adapted her practice to smaller scale projects produced with non-toxic materials—like books. When we met she had a gallery in her apartment called the Mixta Gallery where she offered bookmaking workshops. A few years later we became coworkers at the same community college in Brooklyn, where we both designed syllabi and lesson plans for classes focused on stimulating critical thinking and emotional development. She specialized in arts education and I was taking advantage of the opportunity to share the basics of feminist theory with my students, who were mostly single mothers from Latinx neighborhoods around the city. Tanya made use of lunches, coffee breaks, and free periods to teach me how to make books. With her help, I edited, designed, and published a small run of *Secretos Familiares*, my second poetry collection, a kind of #MeToo testimony ahead of its time. I didn't know it then, but learning to make books would be the key to my whole life.

○

In November 2006 I traveled to Mexico for the first time—to take part in the "Encuentro de Mujeres Poetas en el País de las Nubes," a gathering of women poets in the Sierra Mixteca mountains in Oaxaca. I lost my suitcase at the airport, so I traveled light by necessity. Over the course of the week, I turned twenty-six. I made friends with other women who would go on to become important sources of emotional support and co-creators. I decided, impulsively, to move to Mexico—to write, and walk. The year before, after finishing my Masters degree, I'd chosen not to pursue a doctorate. I felt at odds with the academic environment, and I wanted to learn more about Latin America—beyond the books. I wanted to integrate myself, finally, in "real life." I spent a little more time working in New York and I saved some money. I daydreamed of studying film in Cuba. When the possibility of Mexico came up I had already saved enough to stay there for at least a year without working (thanks to the favorable exchange rate). I enrolled in a creative writing program in Mexico City, but I left that behind too when I realized my education was better served by my everyday interactions—events and conversations with writers of various generations that I got to know on the road.

I began to translate miscellaneous texts online, to make my money last, to trust strangers, to travel wherever I was invited—to live in Mexico day by day. I almost always felt safe, even though I knew that many people suffered horrible violence at the hands of the narcostate. Over time I learned to trust—and refine—my intuition. That first year I didn't even have a cell phone. I adapted to a new rhythm: I learned to take people at their word, to surrender control, and to wait. As cliché as these affirmations may sound, they led me to many waterfalls, towns full of birds with flying bridges, pyramids half-hidden by dense jungle, deserts blooming with peyote, beaches and cenotes where I stripped and swam. And I had friends: friendship acquired a primordial importance. With my new sisters from the poetry festival in Oaxaca, we started to meet in our domestic spaces to read and workshop poems between mezcals.

An Argentine feminist named Miriam Djeordijian managed the CICAM (*Centro de Investigación y Capacitación para la Mujer / Research and Training Center for Women*), a feminist organization in Colonia Roma, and in those years, she began to use the space to host a series of poetry readings for women called "Barcitas." CICAM had published *La correa feminista*, a Latin American journal of feminist thought, for more than ten years.[4] When I began to visit CICAM they were no longer printing the magazine, but the workshop was still there in the back of the kitchen—two Risograph printers, a small offset printer that didn't work, inks, paper remainders, paper cutters, and many other light tools for artisanal publishing. Miriam invited me to reactivate CICAM's press, and as an inaugural gesture I improvised a bookmaking and poetry workshop. Around ten women participated. I didn't have much experience, but I needed to make money somehow and the opportunity excited me. I shared two types of bookbinding I'd learned in New York, and together—with lots of experimentation and technical support from Miriam, who helped us decipher the workshop's tools—we made small runs of poetry books printed on one of the Risographs and bound by hand. This was long before today's golden age of Riso workshops for editorial and graphic design. In fact, I didn't even know the name of the machines we were using. Ten years later, I would realize—thanks to kinetic memory—that the machines at CICAM were exactly the same Risos that I use now in La Impresora. More on that later.

The work is not to think of new things but to make them in a
    different way
The work is not the answer but the problem
The work is the journey not the port of arrival
The work is not the genre but the singularity
The work is not the product but the process
The work is to create spaces of pleasure, of intensity, so that
    desire comes naturally

From "Our Editorial Style,"
La Correa Feminista, Num. 15, 1995

My friends and I began a free poetry workshop that gave us a rhythm for writing and meeting. We borrowed a megaphone from CICAM and formed a kind of sorority that we started to call "Las Poetas del Megáfono."[5] We organized a weekly "open megaphone" in a café in Colonia Roma, where we collectively chose a theme for the next week's poems. Megaphone Tuesdays became a busy hive of experimentation, attracting forty or fifty poets each week, and supporting many different collaborations. Sometimes I like to think we were characters pulled from a little novel Bolaño never published: young women poets living alone in Mexico City and cooking together, sharing clothes, learning to make books learning to make books by hand, buying paper downtown, visiting presses, passing around pirated music on CD's, traveling by bus for hours to get to the beach, performing rudimentary rituals to burn photos of ex-lovers on the rooftop of an apartment building of Salvadoran students on the Calle República de Cuba, very close to Plaza Garibaldi.

I began to attend festivals in Central America that I could reach by bus. I accepted every opportunity that came my way to leave the city and explore towns in Mexico beyond the capital. I camped for whole weeks with people I barely knew and I experienced moments of real connection with the ecosystem and with the road itself. It was a heady time of true freedom, maybe the happiest time of my life. Even though I can see the accumulation of privileges that allowed me to make those choices, I should also point out that back then I had less money and fewer belongings than ever before or since.

The Festival of Navachiste claims a special place in my memories of that period. For more than twenty years, artists and fisher-men have convened over Semana Santa  on a remote beach in Sinaloa full of birds and cactus. The Festival is only reachable by boat, and every person must set up their own camp. They offer a workshop under a palm roof with an invited writer, a poetry contest with modest publication for the winner, a sculpture competition with materials scavenged from the beach, theatrical productions, musical performances, and campfires every night on the shore. The hosts are the local fishermen, who organized the Festival's daily schedule and feed the gathering—often with the catch of the day—in a rustic cafeteria on the sand. With minimal resources, they've created an experience of improbable beauty and resilience. When I imagine my ideal cultural event, I always think of the Festival of Navachiste.

I felt good in Mexico. I was learning things, I had stopped paying my students loans, and I was publishing poetry. The literature my friends and I made was rudimentary, anti-academic, rebellious, political, erotic, without theory, and often naïve. We thought out loud, in the shared dimension we were building one poem at a time. I don't think I had a "project" during this period. I was just connecting the dots. I listened, immersed in a profound process of poetic investigation without any methodology.

The work of the small independent Mexican press Proyecto Literal (who also created the Colección Limón Partido and the Latin American poets' biennial in Mexico City "El Vértigo de los Aires") helped me draw a map of alternative literary production. This Latin American network became aware of itself[6] through the circulation of libros cartoneros,[7] autodidactic bookmaking workshops, and road trips. Alongside the small independent Mexican presses that operated with state subsidies, the cartonera editorial model went viral. The cartonera design and development process was cheap and practical, artisanal but relatively standardized. Even with our shallow poets' pockets, we were able to build a global (or at least Latin

11

American) digital network of autonomous initiatives supporting low-budget local literature, with the help of the internet and the emergence of social media.

In November 2009, while I was still in Mexico, the Puerto Rican poet Xavier Valcárcel and I decided to start a parallel project: Atarraya Cartonera. We were long-distance friends for a few years: we went to the beach together when I was visiting the island, and when I was away we would exchange readings and write poems together by mail. In that way—me in Mexico City and Xavier on the island—we conceptualized our project. We designed three distinct editorial collections: new editions of out of print Puerto Rican poetry, contemporary Puerto Rican poetry, and contemporary Caribbean / Latin American poetry. We also thought of Atarraya Cartonera as an art project. We used cardboard discarded by the multinational bookstore Borders to make covers printed with stencils and spray paint, in dialogue with the political graffiti that proliferated in San Juan. The arrival of Borders in Puerto Rico in 2000 had resulted in the closure and dismantling of many local bookstores; using their trash as our raw material was our critique.[8] During our most active years, we published twenty-five titles made of cardboard and photocopies and organized many bookmaking workshops which, in the midst of the financial crisis,[9] inspired our comrades to explore more accessible avenues of publication. The Puerto Rican publishers were collapsing under the weight of the recession and those that remained were closed circles most responsive to institutional interests, charging the authors large sums to publish their books while excluding them from the editorial process; maybe they still just didn't see our generation as significant cultural producers.

Some time in those days a copy of Ulises Carrión's *El arte nuevo de hacer libros* (*The New Art of Making Books*) fell into my hands, and it became a kind of credo for me. The Mexican poets Inti García Santamaría and Alejandro Albarrán had put a sign up in the empty living room of their new apartment in Colonia Roma —"Multipurpose Room Ulises Carrión"— and they'd begun to host events and poetry readings right there, at home. To celebrate the "inauguration" of the salon, they printed a free, pirated edition of Carrión's already legendary manifesto. Years later I too have photocopied the document Inti gave me and circulated it among friends. The manifesto was not at all new: it had been published for the first time in 1975, in the Mexican magazine *Plural*, edited by Octavio Paz. But for me it was revelatory even thirty-five years later. It felt like a friend's finger pointing the way:

In the new art the writing of the text is only the first link in the chain that goes from writer to reader. In the new art the writer assumes responsibility for the entire process.

In the old art the writer writes texts.
In the new art the writer makes books.[10]

○

The rising cost of rent and public transportation in Mexico City forced me to look for a more cost-effective lifestyle. After a bus trip through the Mayan Riviera—Belize, Guatemala, and Chiapas—I decided to settle down for a while in Chiapas, which gave me the freedom to continue creating with all my necessary digressions. The town of San Cristóbal de las Casas, the cradle of the Zapatista movement,[11] was small enough to navigate on foot, cold enough to keep food fresh without a refrigerator, and slow enough to make time for a coffee with someone any day at any hour—but still cosmopolitan enough to meet people and pursue "projects." I didn't feel ready to return to Puerto Rico yet.

In the summer of 2010 I worked at Taller Leñateros as an interpreter and bilingual guide, receiving visitors that needed attention in English. Taller Leñateros was an artisanal workshop dedicated to the transcription of oral literature from the Mayan people who lived in the surrounding mountain towns. Through the processes of papermaking with natural fibers, traditional bookbinding, and silkscreen printing, they made the most beautiful books I'd ever seen in my life. The workshop had been founded by the American poet Ámbar Past and a group of women from the highlands of Chiapas more than thirty years earlier. It was a model for a form of life guided completely by poetry.

That summer Ámbar and I became friends. From Taller Leñateros I transitioned to helping out in her home workshop, where we conducted experiments with different materials, read poetry out loud, translated poems, and made fires with dry coconuts. Ámbar was also a gardener, and she cultivated a large part of what she ate: on her patio she planted corn, lettuce, cabbage, tomatoes, broad beans, basil, oregano, carrots, daikon radish, chard, arugula, and more. There were also ducks and rabbits that were sacrificed only on special occasions; the rest of the time they supported the cycle of fertilizer and compost and provided eggs for breakfast.

Many people passed through Ámbar's house. She sometimes organized meals on Saturday afternoons for her friends in town and some artist or another who traveled to San Cristóbal to meet her. There were also young Mexican designers and poets who came to do internships with Leñateros or conduct research about her work. But even though the house was full, the scale of things was always small, human, in hand's reach. A profound love of nature breathed through everything that happened there. The presence of her best friend Maruch Mendes, an artist and healer from San Juan Chamula, infused the atmosphere with spiritual depth. Most of the time, in those meetings, Maruch directed her attention only to Ámbar, who spoke Tzotzil fluently and could serve as our interpreter when necessary. The complicity between the two women was a marvel; their friendship impossible to translate.

Gabriela Astorga, the Mexican editor, wrote this about the workshop:

> Founded in 1975 by the U.S. poet Ámbar Past and a group of women from the Chiapas Highlands, the Taller Leñateros was born after Maruch Méndes dreamed that six boys and girls ate a mountain of trash in Ámbar's house. That's how she knew that if they went to work, garbage would bear fruit. And it did for more than thirty years: the workshop became a publisher that was the source of work for two hundred Tzotzil Mayan families that made books and journals totally by hand. They began to make works from the living memory of their communities: the books made in the workshop were the first books to be written, illustrated, and produced by living Mayas in four hundred years.[12]

Being in Chiapas made it possible to establish greater contact with Central American poets, especially in Guatemala and El Salvador. Since Guatemala City was much closer to me than Mexico City, when I wanted to spend time in an urban center that's where I went. I liked visiting the poet Rosa Chávez, who even gave me a copy of her house keys so that I could come and go as I pleased. There I published my book *Añosluz* with an independent press, and I collaborated with Simón Pedroza, an anarchist poet, performer, and master bookmarker who ran editorial workshops out of his garage. Simón's workshop was small, organized, and efficient. Almost all Guatemalan poets had passed through to make artisanal editions of their books under the imprints "s.o.p.a.—sociedad optativa de poetas anónimos (optional society of anonymous poets)" and "ediciones bizarras." Although Simón refused to participate in the official bureaucracies and elite social circles of Guatemalan literature, his cultural work is a point of reference for many artists. Of his publications, I was most marked by *Automátika 9mm*, a butcher paper book made with Javier Payeras and Alejandro Marré: poems, drawings, and lots of blank pages where the reader could intervene, shot through by a bullet hole.

During this period, I also began to play with translating poetry. I had already been translating ordinary documents as a freelancer for a while by then. Translation gave me freedom of movement—I could work long distance from any internet café—just as it now enables me to stay in my house during quarantine and earn a living. I like translation because it allows me to "practice" writing—almost as a performative gesture, a kind of play-acting. Translation maintains my agility: I learn new vocabulary without having to invent the story from scratch. But literary translation seemed pretty intimidating. I had only translated some of my friend's poems into English, but I was interested in translating Latin American poetry for the English market, even though English was not my mother tongue. To overcome my fear, I began to translate collaboratively. In San Cristóbal I met Tom Slingsby, who was living in Chiapas for the year with his wife Tila. Tom worked for Pighog Press—an independent publisher based in Brighton, England—and he proposed making a small bilingual anthology of contemporary Latin American poetry for the

British public. Between coffees, home cooked meals, and long walks through the trees around his wooden house, we translated a selection of sixteen poems together and called it "Hallucinated Horse: New Latin American Poets" after a line from the Chilean poet Javier Norambuena. The anthology was published in 2012, and by that point none of us lived in San Cristóbal. In the translator's note we wrote that "the horse appears like a figure in a dream from a violent past, presaging a swift escape, glimpsed at a crossroads."

II

PUERTO RICO
PARA LOS
PUERTORRISUEÑOS

Esteban Valdés, *Fuera de Trabajo* (QeAse, 1977)[13]

In April 2012, after a season in El Salvador in which the poet Elena Salamanca and I made two books by hand,[14] I came back to Puerto Rico. I arrived in San Juan to mount an installation with Xavier, *Xerografías para una estética contra-neoliberal (Xeroxes for a Counter-Neoliberal Aesthetic)*, an Atarraya commission for the Poly/Graphic Triennial.[15] We published an open call, edited a series of broadsides, published a Puerto Rican poetry anthology about "the crisis,"[16] and planned a program of workshops. I was supposed to stay for at least three months. I was absorbed by a deep enchantment with the island's "green light of mountain and sea,"[17] and even the city began to fascinate me. Almost without thinking, I did not return to Mexico.

I had never lived in San Juan in my adult life, so practically speaking, I was a recent arrival. The writer Alexadra Pagán, a friend of mine since college, recommended that I rent an apartment on Calle Loíza in Santurce's Barrio Machuchal, two blocks from Ocean Park Beach. Machuchal, a former maroon stronghold, is now a diverse district comprised of tourists, artists, a big population of aging seniors, and a large and active Dominican community that maintains the neighborhood's liveliness. Luckily, Calle Loíza has much more pedestrian activity than the rest of the city, where suburbs and traffic reign supreme. Lately it's also become one of San Juan's most gentrified areas. When I first moved in, I took to walking and riding my bicycle and began to discover a city both familiar and unknown. I met like-minded people, I made new friends, and I began to integrate myself into existing projects—to collaborate. The creative scene felt vibrant, diverse, and real. Santurce, the biggest neighborhood of San Juan, was racked by economic ruin but seduced me with its hypnotic, vital pulse. The beach became part of my daily life. The rainforest also became normal. Every day I immersed myself in Puerto Rico's green dimension, the fresh air, the rivers and curves of mountain roads. I swam a lot. I didn't mind staying.

Since I needed to make money while I looked for a job, I organized a few bookmaking workshops in my house where experimental writers and young college students interested in publishing gathered around the table. That same year, with various colleagues, we organized the first

Feria de Libros Independientes y Alternativos-FLIA PR in an empty lot between two buildings on Calle Loíza. I think that was how I became conscious of the scale of my community. At the first FLIA, under the hot sun and without any kind of sponsorship, dozens of independent publishing projects (literary and not) recognized each other as part of the same community, abandoned by institutions but determined to keep creating no matter what. FLIA helped make visible the network that still supports alternative spaces for literature, independent publishing, and art in a country with a lower and lower budget for culture. Alongside many other projects that flourished in the wake of FLIA, Ediciones Aguadulce, MesaEd and Ediciones Alayubia have all published important books of poetry in recent years.[18]

Making a living in Puerto Rico is complicated. The current financial crisis is oppressive in countless ways. Any small business or independent cultural project runs the numbers and is forced to conclude that the natural course is debt or failure. But we still keep trying. A year after my arrival, with that certainty in mind, I debated staying on the island or leaving again for Mexico, where I also didn't have steady work. I didn't really have any place to return to. Ámbar Past was talking about moving to India. In Puerto Rico, on the other hand, I had begun to feel useful. I could give poetry workshops, teach people how to make books, try to mend the illusory breach between writers and editors, and publish around the edges of capitalism. Despite everything, we were all surviving.

In the midst of these considerations, I began a program called "La Práctica" at Beta-Local—a nonprofit organization created by visual artists, dedicated to supporting contemporary art initiatives in Puerto Rico through free programming (lectures, workshops, studio visits, exhibitions, etc.) and residencies hosting local and international artists. Over two years, I went to Beta-Local for weekly meetings with a multidisciplinary group of creators who were, like me, looking for ways to sustain themselves and their artistic practices on the island. The proposal was simple: we would meet, talk, share processes, exchange resources, pool ideas, and advance our "projects," no matter what they were.

From my participation in La Práctica (2013–2015) I highlight the following: Xavier and I celebrated five years of Atarraya Cartonera with an exhibition of works in progress—"intimacies" and "peripheries"[19]—including reference texts, a binder containing printouts of all our e-mails and the stencils we used for the book covers; I organized a series of workshops on free—very free—translation; I had my first "Open Studio," which required me to begin to think of my work in the ritual language of visual art; I took on the production of FLIA and I organized the fifth edition of the fair in 2014; I embarked on the vision, development, and creation of the book *Sucede que yo soy América*; and with the budget set aside for my project I decided to buy a Riso printer and start "something."

Making the book *Sucede que yo soy América* allowed me to synthesize the experiences I'd lived in Mexico, Central America, and New York, sketching out a map of the contemporary Latin American poetry I'd encountered and establishing the foundation of what would soon come to be my publishing project, La Impresora. Connecting the past with the present and the future, the book collected free translations of Allen Ginsberg's poem "America" (first published in California in 1956) by contemporary Latin American poets, along with some of my own reflections and questions about translation. Each one of the poets rewrote, in Spanish, Ginsberg's iconic lines from their own point of view in their present moment: the America of these poems is sometimes Mexico, sometimes Argentina, sometimes Cuba, sometimes Miami, sometimes Colombian New York, sometimes Guatemala, sometimes Panama, sometimes Chile, sometimes Puerto Rico. "American" identity is in constant negotiation, mediated by the power relations between the United States and all the other countries of the hemisphere. For many Latin American poets, Beat poetry is still resonant, for the way it questions North American values, for its search beyond national borders, for the way it's propelled by travel, for its urgent orality. The many recordings of Ginsberg improvising in and around his poem seemed to authorize rewriting. What is "America"? What is "America" from a Latin American perspective? What is translation? What is writing? What does the direction you're translating to/from imply? What is the temporality or validity of a translation? What are its borders and border crossings? Are we going to keep litigating the fidelity of a translation between colonized languages? Are translators also "writers"? What is the degree of authority and creation in this relationship? Those were some of the questions that I asked as I edited *Sucede que yo soy América*. I still haven't found answers.

The first edition of the book was published in collaboration with Circadian Press, the editorial branch of Sacred Bones Records, in Greenpoint, Brooklyn during an institutional residency organized by Beta-Local with the International Studio and Curatorial Program (ISCP) in New York. It was designed by the Chilean artists Felipe Mujica and Johanna Unzueta, who make books as part of their artistic practice. I spent two days in Keegan Cooke's workshop in the basement of a record shop in Brooklyn. Keegan made a living printing album covers and publications commissioned by musicians and artists like Felipe and Johanna. Watching Keegan work alone in that tiny space gave me confidence. There I learned, consciously, to use a Riso, a Vanderbilt press, and a hot melt perfect binder, along with other useful tools. We made one hundred copies of *Sucede que yo soy América*.

In an email sent to the authors in the anthology, dated May 13, 2015, I wrote:

Keegan's workshop / Circadian Press is a dream-like one-man press inside a tiny room in the back of a record shop in Brooklyn. I learned a lot about process and quality control, and I realized I needed many more machines than the ones I have at home right now. In the end we made a run of one hundred copies, but the hot melt machine overheated and a piece broke (it was very hot yesterday in New York) and we couldn't finish more than thirty copies, half of which we distributed and sold yesterday in the presentation at the International Studio and Curatorial Program in Brooklyn. When Keegan repairs the piece and is able to finish binding the books that are left he's going to mail them to me in Puerto Rico and then I will send them to all of you.

The presentation was beautiful and crazy, with a torrent of Spanish and English and an audience that didn't necessarily understand the full scope of the conversation. Urayoán Noel, Diego Rivelino, Nicolás Linares, who are all based in New York, were there, as well as María Tabares and Enrique Winter (who serendipitously were traveling through the city for other reasons and could make it to our event). Even though the conversation about translation emerging from this project could go much deeper, it was beautiful to have the pretext of our relationship with Ginsberg to talk about autobiographical writing, our transits and migrations, the many Spanishes spoken in America, to provoke dialogue among those present with our gaze and our games, and to share a little Puerto Rican rum.

At first, I put the Riso in the back of MAOF Materia y Oficios, a space where the artist Diego de la Cruz (a colleague at La Práctica) was setting up an underground urban sawmill and experimenting with tropical woods and materials not commonly used for construction or local woodworking. MAOF was across the street from the punk bar El Local[20] at bus stop 20 of Avenida Fernández Juncos at the southern end of Santurce, a ruined zone that had been San Juan's commercial center half a century ago. The building was an old sign lettering workshop, recently acquired by developers with an eye for art. Through an agreement with Beta-Local, we installed our workshops there for some time. We shared and negotiated the neighborhood with grafitti artists and vagrants. Abandoned buildings had become informal parking lots. We didn't have to pay rent in MAOF, and that invaluable support cut me some slack to ramble and experiment until La Impresora took shape. Even though it seemed like our

24

projects had nothing to do with one another, Diego was an essential interlocutor. Over several months we got in the habit of starting the day with a bike ride to the beach at El Escambrón, swimming for a while near the reef. We also gathered fruits (mangos, limes, avocados, tamarinds, soursop) from the patios of abandoned houses that we passed on our route. We were reading Ivan Illich out loud and our conversations about communal living, deschooling, tools, speed, and human scale helped me put in perspective what I'd learned with Atarraya Cartonera and what I'd seen in the editorial workshops of Ámbar Past in Chiapas, Simón Pedroza in Guatemala, and Keegan Cooke in New York.

Sofia Gallisá, one of the codirectors of Beta-Local, called us early one morning to go to the old site of Impresora Nacional, a legendary press that had been created as "a business with a socialist foundation" in 1971 to print the weekly newspaper *Claridad*, the official organ of the Pro-Independence Movement and the Puerto Rican Socialist Party.[21] Impresora Nacional had declared bankruptcy and shuttered the year before. Now it was just another warehouse in ruins, with a rotary printer frozen in time, the last page left half-printed. We were welcomed by Carlos Jiménez, one of the old associates, and he told us (with much nostalgia and some resignation) that we could take all the furniture, tools, and materials we wanted. That's where we got the wooden tables that are the heart of our workshop today, and a good amount of paper that we used to print our first publications at La Impresora. In fact, the name "La Impresora" is an homage to Impresora Nacional and to that visit.[22]

On October 29, 2015 I posted this note on my blog, with this photo:

MAOF Materia y oficios

History emerges from each object
What's important are the insignificant moments
Resisting technology's speed
Crafting workshops without teachers
Accompanying ourselves
Learning to be
Communicating with passing birds
Exhibition of usefulness
Repetition as an opportunity to be with yourself

At the end of the year I had the opportunity to return to Mexico for the first time since I'd moved to Puerto Rico. I did a residency focused on editorial production at the Cooperativa Editorial Cráter Invertido, in the neighborhood of Colonia San Rafael in Mexico City, where I produced the second edition of *Sucede que yo soy América* and learned some of the administrative aspects of operating a Riso workshop. We made five hundred copies of the book, the biggest run I'd worked on up until that point. My friend Marina Ruiz, who had also been part of the Poetas del Megáfono collective, helped me print and bind the books. Now she was directing the artisanal press Astrolabio in Cuernavaca. Between serendipity and luck, this trip coincided with the first RRRéplica, a conference for "disobedient presses" where I made connections with other publishers using Risograph printers. This experience renovated and redefined the terms of my relationship with Mexico. I always try to visit with some frequency to catch up with friends, exchange books, buy materials, recharge, and rest from the daily struggle of life in Puerto Rico.

Presentation of the second edition of *Sucede que yo soy América* in the public library of Aeromoto in Mexico City, January 21, 2016.

○

In January of 2016 the poet Amanda Hernández came into my life to do an internship with La Impresora as part of her Master's in Cultural Administration and from that moment on we've worked side by side, building up the workshop along the way. We won some grants that helped us buy the rest of the equipment and tools we needed for our setup and we taught ourselves to use them through trial and error. On a one-year contract with the city of San Juan, we developed a free program of recurring presentations and workshops for all ages organized through FLIA and the Casa de Cultura Ruth Hernández Torres, a vibrant space in Río Piedras that reached a high point under the direction of the multidisciplinary artist Gisela Rosario Ramos. We also began to print projects and publications for the artists in the Beta-Local network and to define the services we could offer to guarantee the sustainability of La Impresora. Little by little we began to publish books of poetry. 2016 was a year of evanescent prosperity, just before the PROMESA law imposed new, asphyxiating austerity measures affecting every aspect of Puerto Rican life.[23]

We were at MAOF until May 2017. The owners had new plans for the building and we had to leave. With the generous help of friends, we moved La Impresora to our current studio on the famous Calle Calma, in Barrio Machuchal, which is also the neighborhood where Amanda and I live, a few blocks from each other. Calle Calma is, as they say, the "backroom" of Calle Loíza: this part of the neighborhood, the poorest and most stigmatized, is known for being the birthplace of the great salsero Ismael Rivera and an enclave of Puerto Rican popular music from rumba to reggaeton. Our friend and neighbor Lío Villahermosa (a multidisciplinary artist and bomba dancer) grew up here, and he offered to rent his family's empty apartment, betting on our ability to keep the project afloat and our shared dedication to the local community.

Grateful and enthusiastic, we began to make ourselves at home in the neighborhood, which turned out to be much more hospitable than Avenida Fernández Juncos.[24]

In June of that year we organized "Edit: Encuentro de gestión editorial independiente" (Edit: A Gathering of Independent Publishers) in collaboration with Beta-Local, with the intention of seeding a conversation among colleagues about editing, publishing, and circulating materials responsive to our particular realities. Various Mexican projects participated alongside some of the independent publishers that regularly presented at FLIA. Although we would've liked more local participation, there still remains work to be done to bridge the divide between the world of visual art (represented by Beta-Local, the site of the event) and other cultural development efforts, including literary publishing.

A few months later Hurricane Maria hit.

Without electricity, amid rubble and widespread confusion, we were able to temporarily relocate the Riso to El Almacén, a garage in the barrio of Trastalleres (also in Santurce) where a friend wanted to start a hackerspace. Javier Rodríguez, musician and inventor, was repairing a good number of broken solar panels that had flown off in the storm. In this way, he was able to establish a small power grid. Faced with the urgency of finding communal solutions to the disaster we were living through, he invited various friends to work from El Almacén for a few weeks and use the solar panels in exchange for helping him reanimate the space and keep him company. We took the

Riso and began to do "solar Riso." There wasn't much work for obvious reasons, but all the same we were able to print a few things from there. Those hot and terrible months we were forced to consider, again and again, why we were doing the work we were doing.

First, we ratified our choice in favor of manual labor, small tools, and analog processes. Thanks to the nature of this work (and the support of El Almacén, which allowed us to plug in the Riso for two or three hours a week), we could keep binding books on Calle Calma, more or less like we'd done before, without depending on electricity. Keeping our hands busy buoyed our spirits, even though we weren't making a profit and outside everything was destroyed. We also decided to slow down the rhythm of our commercial printing services and look for a way to subsidize the publication of poetry, our project's main objective. We applied for emergency funds and grants to make books in line with our main editorial objectives; we published personal projects; both of us wrote our own poetry. At the urging of our friends—poets, editors, illustrators, and artists—we reactivated FLIA in makeshift form, even though we didn't have a budget to produce it, as a pretext to gather together around our books.

Even though the disasters have continued to accumulate around us, we fight, alongside many other people, to adapt to our changing circumstances and continue to make poetry and books available locally in Puerto Rico. We try to facilitate spaces where we can share, create, and learn a craft that isn't taught in any of the island's universities. La Impresora now functions almost like an informal school of poetry and editorial skills. Each book we make testifies to a process of collaboration: editing, design, and production. We make poetry books as well as comics, gallery catalogs, prints by local illustrators, signs for marches, and flyers for events and concerts. We offer workshops in Riso printing, creative writing, and bookbinding. We organize readings and literary events. Our space has been a refuge for friends and young artist-writers whose educational opportunities and general life chances are more threatened every year by budget cuts, political corruption, climate change, and a growing sense of insecurity and uncertainty. Under these circumstances, we've becomes facilitators and workers in a network of processes and exchanges centering on the independent creation of books on an island in crisis. I've come to think that the books we make by hand are not properly commodities, but rather points of encounter that adapt and circulate among our communities under another more noble, more fluid logic. Personally, poetry is what drives me.

June 2020
San Juan, Puerto Rico

References

1   Dorothea Lasky, *Poetry Is Not a Project*, Ugly Duckling Presse, 2010. Available Online: https://issuu.com/uglyducklingpresse/docs/poetry_is_not_a_project_ebook

2   https://en.wikipedia.org/wiki/Stone_Soup

3   An obituary I wrote for him is here: "Mural Writing: Stolen Flowers for the Lower East Side Poet." July 8, 2011. https://www.80grados.net/escritura-mural/

4   https://archivos-feministas.cieg.unam.mx/publicaciones/la_correa_feminista.html

5   Las Poetas del Megáfono was a collective of women writers based in Mexico City that was most active between 2008 and 2020, formed by: Lauri García Dueñas (El Salvador), María Tabares (Colombia), Eva Cabo, (Galicia), Marina Ruiz (Cuernavaca), Diana Reza (Guanajuato), Anaïs Abreu (Mexico City), Ximena de Tavira (Mexico City), Haydée Ramos Cadena (Mexico City) and me. At least three of us have continued to explore the work of handmade books and have developed alternative editorial projects in the decade following our collaboration.

6   In addition to the "Poetas del Megáfono" that I already named, more people in this network are: Jocelyn Pantoja (México, editor of Limón Partido), Héctor Hernández Montecinos (Chile), Yaxkin Melchy (México), Luis Méndez Salinas and Carmen Lucía Alvarado (editors of Catafixia Editorial in Guatemala), Ernesto Carrión (Ecuador), Elena Salamanca (El Salvador), Javier Norambuena (Chile), Enrique Winter (Chile), Rosa Chávez (Guatemala), Wingston González (Guatemala),

Jamila Medina (Cuba), Ámbar Past (Chiapas), Mariana Rodríguez (Chiapas), Mara Pastor (Puerto Rico), Gerardo Grande (Ciudad de México), Manuel Barrios (Uruguay), Javier Alvarado (Panamá), Simón Pedroza (Guatemala), just to name a few.

7   Xavier Valcárcel writes: "As the popular phenomenon we know today, *cartoneras* originated in Buenos Aires, Argentina in March 2003, at an inflection point of financial crisis that began around 1998 and pushed millions into an informal subsistence economy. The seed project, called *Eloísa Cartonera*, defined the terms of the movement. That project gave a name to the kind of alternative editorial project that produces books cheaply using artisanal methods, with pieces of cardboard, spray paint, photocopies, needle and thread or staples, as part of anti-capitalist proposition. As a DIY literary and artistic form, the *cartonera* movement confronts not only the political crisis of social life, but also contemporary editorial frameworks subject to the push and pull of capitalism and globalization." Available online: https://mapacultural.wordpress.com/2011/02/22/gestar-cultura-y-re-sistencia-cartoneras-atarraya-cartonera-y-una-residencia-artisti-ca-en-el-museo-de-arte-contemporaneo-de-puerto-rico/

8   Borders closed its stores in Puerto Rico in 2011, but the local circuit of bookstores still hasn't recovered from the impact.

9   "During the past two decades, this US territory was plunged into a deep economic recession as tax incentives for foreign companies were phased out. Companies left in droves in search of less regulation and greater corporate welfare. Almost immediately unemployment started to increase, public coffers dwindled, residents were told to tighten their belts, and many began migrating in greater numbers in search of economic stability and opportunity. Puerto Rico's public

33

debt, which eventually grew to more than $72 billion, helped lay the groundwork that made Hurricane Maria so devastating and the recovery so slow. The debt ballooned as Puerto Rican officials turned to Wall Street to address the economic stagnation that followed corporate flight, increasingly taking on greater debt in an attempt to stay afloat. (...) As a result about one-third of Puerto Rico's budget is now funneled toward servicing a debt that many believe is both unconstitutional and unsustainable." Yarimar Bonilla and Marisol LeBrón, "Introduction," *Aftershocks of Disaster*, Haymarket Books, 2019, p. 5–6.

10   Ulises Carrión, "El arte nuevo de hacer libros," in *Plural*, no. 41, Mexico City, February 1975. Available online: https://monoskop.org/images/f/f6/Carrion_Ulises_1975_El_arte_nuevo_de_hacer_libros.pdf

11   See T. Olesen, "The Zapatistas and Transnational Framing", in *Latin American Social Movements: Globalization, Democratization, and Transnational Networks* (Eds. Hank Johnston and Paul Almeida), Rowman & Littlefield 2006; and correspondence with EZLN. Available online: https://palabra.ezln.org.mx/

12   Gabriela Astorga, #White Whales, "In my mother's womb I dream spells." Cantos de las leñateras tzotziles, NoFM Radio, 2018. Although one of the most valuable legacies of pre-Colombian Mayan culture was precisely its great volume of codices and books, the oppression of five hundred years of colonization has relegated these communities to extreme poverty, illiteracy, and silence. Their culture, literature, and customs have survived thanks to a potent sense of resilience, under the safeguard of the oral tradition. The books made in Taller Leñateros take pride in being the first Mayan books published since the ancient codices.

13   This concrete poem by Esteban Valdés takes the anticolonial rallying cry "PUERTO RICO PARA LOS PUERTORRIQUEÑOS"— "PUERTO RICO FOR PUERTO RICANS"—in a surreal, utopic direction by substituting the ending -QUEÑOS with the rhyming word -SUEÑOS. His poem claims Puerto Rico for Puerto Ricans, yes, but specifically for the *dreams* that Puerto Ricans have for a different, still-to-be-manifested future. [*Translator's note.*]

14   I helped Elena Salamanca begin the publishing project París-Volcán and together we made her book *San Salvador* and my book *Poemas para megáfono*. We printed small silkscreens for the covers, and the books were hand-stitched using Japanese bookbinding.

15   "La *Trienal Poli/Gráfica de San Juan* in an official cultural project of the Puerto Rican government, produced by the Institute of Puerto Rican Culture and coordinated by its Fine Arts Program. From its first installment, the event has affirmed its pledge to promote graphic art and its evolution through relevant approaches to traditional practice, embracing the innovations made possible by current technology." Xavier Valcárcel in "Cartoneras: Máquinas culturales alternas de producción editorial," unpublished.

16   Various authors, *Plomos: Antolwogía* (Eds. Nicole Delgado and Xavier Valcárcel), Atarraya Cartonera, 2012. Available online: https://drive.google.com/file/d/1XTH0Xo0HPXOUggNCgMeCfINZ 1kxY9rI9/view

17   "Verde luz de monte y mar" is a line from the popular song "Verde Luz," composed by Puerto Rican songwriter Antonio Cabán Vale "El Topo" in 1966, which is commonly known as the "second national anthem" of Puerto Rico.

18   Independent and artisanal publishing is not a new phenomenon in Puerto Rico and it has been especially important for poetry. For example, there's the important editorial work of the publisher QeAse in the 1970s, led by the poets Joserramón Meléndes and Esteban Valdés, who published many of the most significant poetry books of that time including *Animal fiero y tierno* by Anjelamaría Dávila, *Fuera de trabajo* by Esteban Valdés (the first book of concrete poetry in Puerto Rico), *La sílaba en la piel* by José María Lima, and Antolojía de la sospecha, a unique map of the period's young poets. In fact, *Fuera de trabajo* by Estebán Valdés has just been republished in a facsimile edition (Beta-Local/Taller de ediciones económicas, 2020), along with an in-depth interview with the author where he speaks in detail about the creation of the independent press and the publication process behind those books. It's also worth mentioning another example: much of the work of the national poet Juan Antonio Corretjer (1908–1985) originally circulated in small chapbooks and stays in print in modest artisanal reprints published by the Fundación Casa Corretjer.

19   https://betalocal.org/5-anos-de-atarraya-cartonera/

20   For a succinct and relevant review of the role of the punk bar El Local on the musical scene and underground cultural life of San Juan in recent years, see: Cintrón Arbasetti, Joel. *El Local*. Serie Literatura Hoy, Instituto de Cultura Puertorriqueña, 2016.

21   Palau Suárez, Awilda. *Veinticinco años de Claridad*. Editorial de la Universidad de Puerto Rico. 1992.

22   Although Impresora Nacional shut down operations in 2014, the weekly paper *Claridad*, whose slogan is "The Newspaper of the Puerto Rican Nation," still publishes regularly and is one of the primary homes

for investigative journalism, critical thought, and cultural diffusion in Puerto Rico. Available online: https://www.claridadpuertorico.com/

23   In the summer of 2015, then Governor Alejandro García Padilla declared that Puerto Rico's extraordinarily high debt was "unpayable." This led the U.S. Congress to develop a law, called the Puerto Rico Oversight, Management, and Economic Stability Act (PROMESA), to restructure the public debt in Puerto Rico in the coming year, under the mandate of a Fiscal Control Board that was not elected by the people, obviously inclined to protect the economic interests of Wall Street brokers, to dismantle the public sphere, and advance an aggressive agenda of privatization and austerity. See: Ed Morales, "Puerto Rico's Unjust Debt" and Eva Prados-Rodríguez, "Puerto Rico's Fight for a Citizen Debt Audit: A Strategy for Public Mobilization and a Fair Reconstruction", *Aftershocks of Disaster* (Eds. Yarimar Bonilla and Marisol LeBrón), Haymarket Books, 2019.

24   La Impresora is not alone in Barrio Machuchal. We inhabit the many complexities of the neighborhood alongside diverse artistic projects, independent workshops, and community-based initiatives. In recent years, the work of the Taller-Comunidad La Goyco stands out as an important example: a former school that was closed by the government in 2015 but has been reclaimed by a group of neighbors to create a community cultural center. Today La Goyco fulfills an important social function in the area, offering aid to the elderly population, artistic programming for all ages, among many other services attending to immediate needs as they arise day to day. It is, above all, a meeting place and relief center for the community in a neighborhood squeezed more and more tightly by gentrification and disaster capitalism.

A Mano / By Hand
Copyright © Nicole Cecilia Delgado, 2020
Translation Copyright © Carina del Valle Schorske, 2020

The author is especially grateful to her friends and colleagues Javier Norambuena, Raquel Salas Rivera, Alexandra Pagán, Xavier Valcárcel, Francisco Félix, Carina del Valle Schorske, Pablo Guardiola, Karla Claudio Betancourt, Ámbar Past, Rebekah Smith and Melanie Pérez Ortiz, who read and revised earlier drafts of this text.

2020 Pamphlet Series
ISBN 978-1-946433-49-7
First Edition, First Printing
Edition of 1,000

Ugly Duckling Presse
The Old American Can Factory
232 Third Street, #E-303
Brooklyn, NY 11215
uglyducklingpresse.org

Distributed in the USA by SPD/Small Press Distribution
Distributed in the UK by Inpress Books

Series design by chuck kuan and Sarah Lawson
Typeset by Wen Zhuang
Type is New Century Schoolbook
Cover paper and flyleaf from French Paper Co.
Printed offset and bound at McNaughton & Gunn
Flyleaf printed letterpress at Ugly Duckling Presse

This publication was made possible in part by the New York State Council on the Arts, a state agency. This project is supported by the Robert Rauschenberg Foundation.

This pamphlet is part of UDP's 2020 Pamphlet Series: twenty commissioned essays on poetics, translation, performance, collective work, pedagogy, and small press publishing. The authors are listed below; their pamphlets are available for individual purchase and as a subscription (uglyducklingpresse.org/subscribe). Each offers a different approach to the pamphlet as a form of working in the present, an engagement at once sustained and ephemeral.

Mirene Arsanios

Omar Berrada*

Sergio Chejfec

Don Mee Choi

Kunci Study Forum & Collective

Iris Cushing

Simon Cutts

Nicole Cecilia Delgado

Adjua Gargi Nzinga Greaves

Dimitra Ioannou

Sibyl Kempson

Claudia La Rocco

Aditi Machado

Chantal Maillard

Tinashe Mushakavanhu

Sawako Nakayasu

Tammy Nguyen

Aleksandr Skidan

Steven Zultanski

Magdalena Zurawski

*Nadine George-Graves & Okwui Okpokwasili

To win a subscription, write to office@uglyducklingpresse.org with your solution to the following puzzle: Using only 6 straight lines, divide the circle on the back cover so that each number is in its own section, without any overlap between numbers.